A flame is carried from Olympia to the host city. It is symbolic of the ancient games, when relay racers passed a flaming torch instead of a baton.

The torch is lit using the sun and a mirror. It has travelled around the world by steamboat and sledge and by canoe and camel. Whatever next?

Published
by Hogs Back
Books Ltd, The Stables,
Down Place, Hogs Back,
Guildford, GU3 1DE.
Copyright Hogs Back Books
2012. Illustrations copyright
Zack McLaughlin 2012.
Printed in China.
ISBN 9781907432125

O
is for
Olympics

Ned Elliott
Zack McLaughlin

Spanish paralympic archer, Antonio Rebo... fired a flaming arro... to light the Olymp... flame at the 1992 Olympics.

A is for Athletics

Athens hosted the first moder... international Olym... in 1896. Athletes f... 12 nations took p... Today, more tha... 200 countries a... represented.

Cock and bull – the finest badminton shuttlecocks are said to be made from the feathers of the left wing of a goose.

The art of boxing at the ancient Olympics was to avoid being hit. One fighter escaped blows for two days before his worn out opponent gave up.

B is for Bullseye

C

is for Cycling

The first Olympic Road Race in 1896 went from Athens to Marathon, and back again. Six cyclists took part. Today more than 200 compete.

Old Nag? In 1972, 70-year-old British rider Lorna Johnstone became the oldest women to compete at the Olympic Games - 190 in horse years!

E

is for

Equestrian

En garde! After the 1924 Games, the Italian and Hungarian fencing teams settled a scoring dispute with a real-life duel.

From zero to hero – Emperor Nero fell from his chariot at the Games in AD 67, but was declared the winner anyway.

F

is for

Flame

G

is for Gymnastics

Gold medals weren't awarded until 1904. Winner Paris in 1900 recei paintings instead the French thoug they were more valuable.

'Gymnastics' comes from the Greek word 'gymnos', meaning 'nude'; whilst 'hockey' comes from the French 'hocquet' for a 'shepherd's crook'.

H is for Hoplite

The final and toughest race in the ancient Olympic games involved athletes carrying the weapons and armour of a hoplite soldier.

I is for Ideal

The Olympic ideal holds that individuals, not countries, are free to compete against each other in sport.

J

is for
Javelin

Hercules, son of Zeus, was said to be the first **javelin** thrower. In ancient times, competitors threw javelins at a target whilst riding.

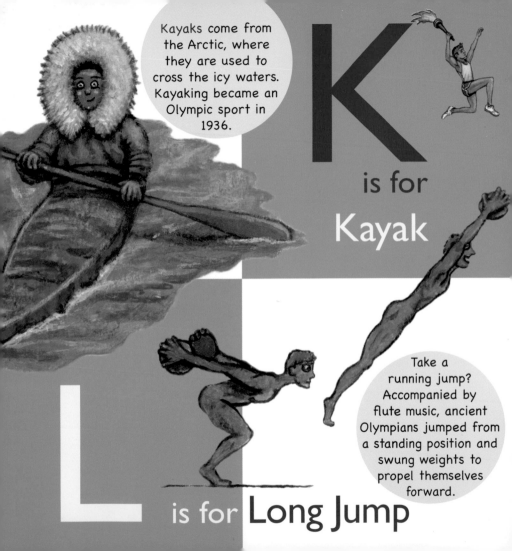

Kayaks come from the Arctic, where they are used to cross the icy waters. Kayaking became an Olympic sport in 1936.

K

is for

Kayak

Take a running jump? Accompanied by flute music, ancient Olympians jumped from a standing position and swung weights to propel themselves forward.

L

is for **Long Jump**

Pheidippides ran 42km from Marathon to Athens in 490 BC, with news of Greece's victory over Persia. The marathon is run over the same distance.

M is f

N is fo

Nike

Nike, Greek goddess of victory, was sent by Zeus to crown the winners at the ancient games. She now appears on all Olympic medals.

Marathon

Lorz unto himself - in 1904, Fred Lorz was about to receive the gold medal when it was discovered that he'd travelled 17km of the marathon by car.

All athletes in Olympia competed in the nude. Only men took part and any married women caught watching were hurled from a cliff.

O is for Olympia

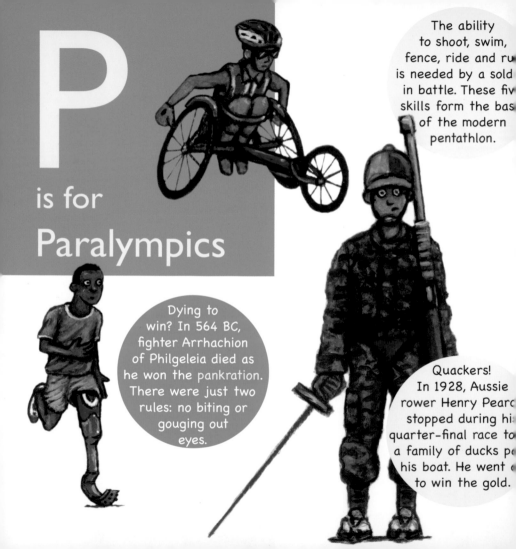

P

is for

Paralympics

The ability to shoot, swim, fence, ride and run is needed by a soldier in battle. These five skills form the basis of the modern pentathlon.

Dying to win? In 564 BC, fighter Arrhachion of Philgeleia died as he won the pankration. There were just two rules: no biting or gouging out eyes.

Quackers! In 1928, Aussie rower Henry Pearce stopped during his quarter-final race to let a family of ducks pass his boat. He went on to win the gold.

Q

is for
Quadrennial

The games are a quadrennial (four-yearly) event and are hosted by different cities around the world.

R

is for
Rings

S is for Stadium

A sport for men in the 1800s, synchronised swimming is now one of just two women-only Olympic events. The other is rhythmic gymnastics.

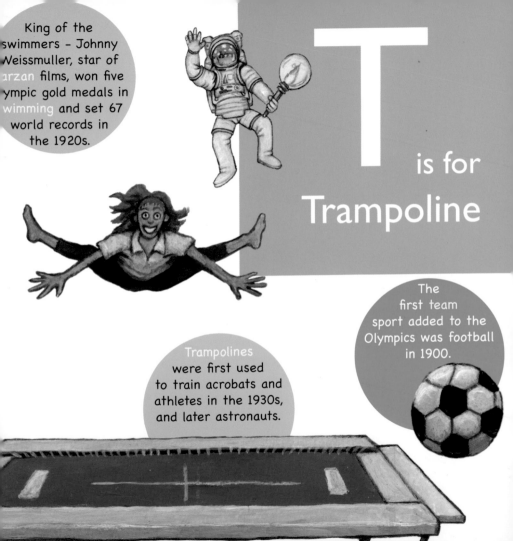

King of the swimmers – Johnny Weissmuller, star of Tarzan films, won five Olympic gold medals in swimming and set 67 world records in the 1920s.

T is for Trampoline

Trampolines were first used to train acrobats and athletes in the 1930s, and later astronauts.

The first team sport added to the Olympics was football in 1900.

U is for

Underwater Swimming

Pull the other one! Along with underwater swimm other discontinue events include tug war, rope climbi and pigeon shooting.

Underwater swimmers earned points for the time and distance swum underwater. It wasn't great fun to watch, so was dropped from later games.

V is for Volleyball

Pole vaulting originated in Holland and the east coast of England, where people used a pole to cross canals and marshy land.

W is for Wreath

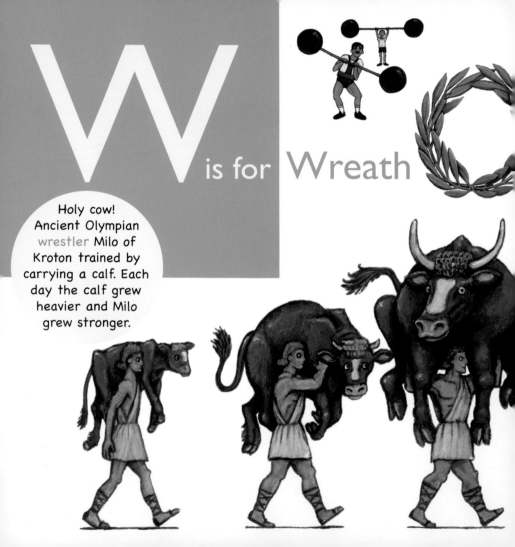

Holy cow! Ancient Olympian wrestler Milo of Kroton trained by carrying a calf. Each day the calf grew heavier and Milo grew stronger.

BMX was created by Californian children in the 1960s as their version of motocross. It has grown up to be a full Olympic sport.

X is for

XXX Olympiad

The XXX (30th) Olympiad in London was the third to be hosted by the city. It spanned 17 days. The 1908 London event continued for 187 days (10x longer).

Y
is for Yachting

Oh buoy –
Ralph Craig ran
in the 100m for the
US in 1912. He returned
to the Olympics in the
US yachting team
36 years later in
1948.

Z is for Zeus

The ancient games were held to honour Zeus – god of sky and thunder. His statue in Olympia was one of the Seven Wonders of the World.

Athletes found cheating at Olympia were fined. The money was used to build statues, called Zanes, which lined the route to the stadium.

O

is for

Olympics

Find out more fascinating facts about
the Olympics at
www.oisforolympics.com

Look out for L is for London and
for more books in our
A is for Alphabet
series coming soon.

Hogs Back Books – a nose for a good book

A a – Athletics
B b – Bullseye
C c – Cycling
D d – Dream
E e – Equestrian
F f – Flame
G g – Gymnastics
H h – Hoplite

I i – Ideal
J j – Javelin
K k – Kayak
L l – Long jump
M m – Marathon
N n – Nike
O o – Olympia